Living Near a Volcano

Written by Kerrie Shanahan

Flying Start
to Literacy®

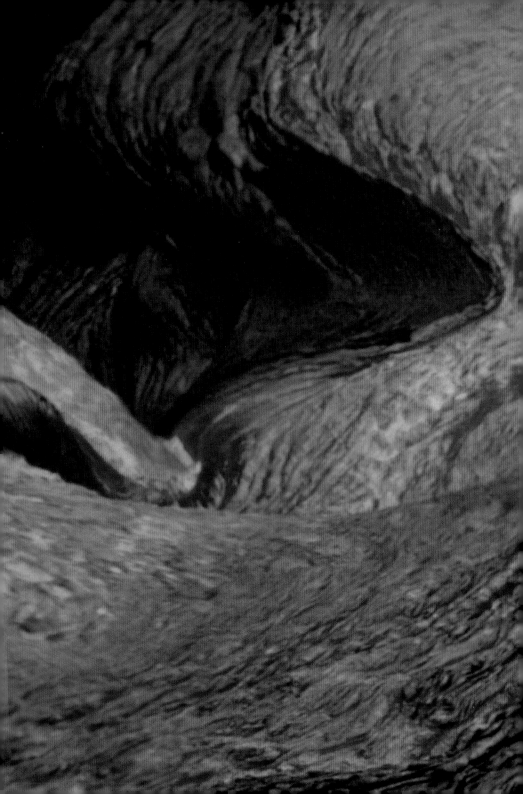

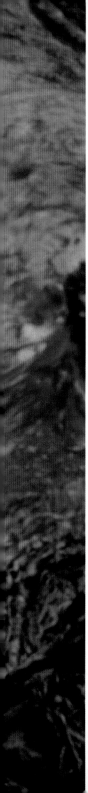

Contents

Mount Etna

Mount Etna is a large volcano in Italy.

It is an active volcano and it could erupt at any time.

Mount Etna is one of the most active volcanoes in the world. The top of Mount Etna nearly always has smoke, ash and molten rock called lava coming out of it.

Living near Mount Etna

Thousands of people live on or near Mount Etna, even though it is a dangerous place.

These people live and work on farms and in villages and towns nearby.

People have farms near the volcano because the soil around the volcano is very good for growing crops. The farmers can sell their crops in the towns and villages nearby.

The soil is very fertile because it has a lot of ash and minerals. The ash and minerals come from the volcano.

Most of the time, people who live near Mount Etna are safe.

But the people who live near Mount Etna know what to do when the volcano is about to erupt. They need to be ready to evacuate the farms, villages and towns and go to a safe place.

When Mount Etna erupts

When Mount Etna erupts,
rocks, ash and smoke
are thrown into the air.
The rocks crash down
the sides of the mountain.

Rivers of lava flow out of the volcano and down the sides of the mountain. The lava is so hot that it burns everything it flows over.

When the lava cools down, it becomes hard rock. Anything that the lava has flowed over and covered is then trapped in the hard rock.

Predicting eruptions

In the past, people did not know when Mount Etna was about to erupt. When the volcano erupted, it caused a lot of damage and killed thousands of people.

Today, scientists are able to predict
when Mount Etna is going to erupt.
They can measure changes on the
mountain. They leave instruments
on the mountain to collect information
about the volcano.

Keeping safe

Scientists send out an alert
when they know that the
volcano is going to erupt.
This gives people time to
leave or to protect
their towns.

Some people made a wall
of rocks to stop the lava
from flowing over their town.
This wall made the lava
flow away from the town.

The town was saved.

rock and gravel wall

lava

The next eruption

Mount Etna will erupt again, but no one knows exactly when this will happen. Scientists believe that it could happen one day soon.

Scientists check for tremors under the ground and for any changes in the volcano. This can tell them if Mount Etna is about to erupt.

Scientists are confident that, with this information, people will have time to evacuate safely.

Glossary

active   an active volcano that is likely to erupt at any time

alert   a message that tells people what is happening

ash   very fine particles of rock that come out of a volcano during an eruption

eruption   when lava, steam and ash come out of a volcano

evacuate   to leave when there is danger

fertile   able to produce a lot of new growth

instruments tools that are used to measure movements and tremors

lava hot molten rock that erupts from a volcano

minerals something that is formed naturally under the ground

molten melted by heat

tremor when the ground shakes

volcanic made by volcanoes, e.g. volcanic ash, volcanic rock

volcano a hole in the earth's crust that lava, steam and ash can erupt from

Index